Soccer...Football?!?

original story:
Jennifer Degenhardt

translator: Susan López

editor: Grant Collins

cover artist: Alex Duarte

All rights reserved. No part of this publication may be reproduced, stored in a retrieval system, or transmitted in any form or by any means - electronic, mechanical, photocopying, recording or otherwise – without prior written permission of the authors, except for brief passages quoted by a reviewer in a newspaper, magazine or blog. To perform any of the above is an infringement of copyright law.

Copyright © 2023 Jennifer Degenhardt
(Puentes)
All rights reserved.
ISBN: 978-1-956594-38-6

For Steve, Rob & A.J.
Most of what I know about football,
I learned from you.

CONTENTS

Acknowledgments	i
Chapter 1 - Martin	1
Chapter 2 - Coach Albano	5
Chapter 3 - Jamal	11
Chapter 4 - Martin	16
Chapter 5 - Coach Albano	21
Chapter 6 - Jamal	26
Chapter 7 - Martin	33
Chapter 8 - Jamal	37
Chapter 9 - Coach Albano	41
Chapter 10 - Martin	46
Chapter 11 - Narrator	54
About the Author	59
About the Translator	63
About the Cover Artist	64
About the Student Liaison	65
About the Editor	66

ACKNOWLEDGMENTS

In what seems like a lifetime ago, I was fortunate to be included as a member of the football coaching staff for three different high schools. At first, I did little more than hang out on the sideline, but by the third gig, I was filming and even did a little scouting. Through my experiences, I learned so much - not only about the game of football, but about what it really means to be part of team. So, to Steve Filippone, Rob Trifone and A.J. Albano, thanks for letting me hang out with you all.

In the fall of 2022, I attended NYSAFLT's statewide conference in Rochester, NY, where I was so fortunate to meet Gracia Guzmán, a world language coordinator on Long Island, who works primarily with newcomer English language learners (ELLs). Gracia was lovely enough to chat with me for a while where I was able tell her how much I enjoy working with students. Like I do, Gracia wants to provide opportunities for her students. She suggested Susan López and Alex Duarte to translate and do the artwork for this story. Thank you, Gracia, for your efforts in coordinating the connection between the students and me.

The four of us met via Zoom, where the students were able to ask me any questions about the project. Both students were committed from the start and were a pleasure to work with. Thank you, to Susan for her bilingual skills which she used to translate this story. And thank you, to Alex, for his beautiful artwork. I am grateful for their work - even more so since football isn't exactly the most popular sport in their cultures. ☺

Grant Collins was instrumental with editing the sports language throughout the story. It was a challenge to write a story about football in comprehensible Spanish to begin with, but to then have that comprehensible language sound convincing in English is a whole different ball game (pun intended). As a sports aficionado, during his senior year, Grant founded the first sports reporting outlet for his high school, for which he wrote most of the articles. The choice of Grant to edit this story was a no-brainer, as they say. Grant, thank you for your help to make the story that much more readable sports-wise.

Chapter 1
Martin

The coach blows the whistle to indicate the end of practice.

"Come on boys! Pack up the balls."

All the boys are tired because of the long, three-hour practice. We walk slowly to where the coach is standing, near the goal.

"Hustle up!" he tells us.

The boys begin to jog towards the coach.

"Sit down."

All the boys sit on the turf.

"As all of you know, today I will announce the teams for varsity and junior varsity.

The coach starts reading the last names of the boys that will make up the varsity team.

- Silva
- Jones

- Gallagher
- Martinez
- Donoghue

The coach reads sixteen last names in total, for the varsity team.

"Go to the locker room and get ready for our first practice tomorrow as a team."

Ah! I'm not in the first group, but that's okay. I'm still in 9th grade and I'm not that big.

But I really want to be part of the soccer program. I have been playing soccer for eight years.

I want to hear my name.

"Now I'll announce the names of the boys who will make up the junior varsity team."

The coach reads fifteen last names.

- Rodriguez
- Salazar
- Collins

- Miller
- Bassaragh

He reads fifteen last names, but not mine.

"Go with Mr. Sheldon. He will talk to you about being on the junior varsity team. The rest of you, thank you for coming out, please try again next year."

With those words, the head coach of the varsity team turns around and starts walking towards the school.

With those words, I believe I have a problem.

I'm not part of the soccer program? Am I not going to continue to play my favorite sport?

I can't think right now.

How am I going to explain this to my father?

Being a soccer player on the school team has been my father's dream for me for many years.

He loves soccer. He wants me to play at an advanced level.

But right now, I'm not playing at any level.

I take the soccer ball out from my backpack and start to knock it around[1]. I rip a shot[2] towards the goal.

In my mind I hear my father's voice: "kick it harder."

I run to get the ball and shoot it again.

I shoot the ball for an hour.

How am I going to explain this situation to my father?

---
[1] knock it around: kick the ball.
[2] rip a shot: kick the ball.

Chapter 2
Coach Albano

In one week, our team has its first game.

Normally I'm really, really excited for opening day, but this year it's a little different.

I think back to the email I received from the head of the board of education.

> **Steve:**
>
> **Win the first game. You don't have a choice. If you don't, someone else is going to get your position.**
>
> **Nik Moulton**

It's not a threat, but a promise. Nik Moulton is very serious. He likes football; no, he loves football. His son plays on our team.

I don't want to think about the email.

I have to think about the new plays and players we have this year.

I blow the whistle to indicate the end of practice. Tweet! Tweet!

"Okay guys, pack up the equipment," I tell them.

The players pick up the balls, sleds, tackling dummies, and tees.

We practiced special teams today: kickoff, field goal, and extra-point or PAT[3]. Every one of those plays require a kick.

Every one of those plays requires a player with a strong leg.

And of the almost fifty players on the team...no one has a strong leg.

"Good job today, boys." I tell them. "We have one more week to get ready for our first game. We're playing on the road against the San Marcos Academy. They're a good football team. We can win, but we have to be prepared and..."

---

[3] PAT: point after touchdown.

I look at all the players. They are athletic and strong, but none of them can kick.

"...we need a kicker. Of the almost fifty players on the team, none of you can kick," I tell them. "But that's my problem. Go to the locker room. Get changed and head to the film room. We're going to watch the San Marcos's defense."

All the players walk to the locker room. I talk to the other coaches.

"How is it that no one on this team can kick?"

"It's not a good situation, Steve," a coach says.

"We have to find a kicker. It's necessary for us to win this season," I tell them. I think back to the email, and the threat. "Okay. See you in the film room, I have to get my things."

I walk over to where my things are, by the goalposts. From the corner of my eye, I see a boy kicking soccer balls at the goal. He's really far from the goal, but the ball goes in every time he kicks it.

Could he be our kicker? No, he's a soccer player..."

I walk over to where he is.

"Hey," I say to him. "You have a strong leg. You're really talented."

The boy looks at me. He's not happy, but still answers me.

"Yeah, I can kick really well, and maybe I am talented... but not enough to be a part of the team."

"What are you saying? You're not a soccer player?" I ask him.

"Not anymore. I'm not part of the team... My father is going to be really mad," the boy says to me.

"What's your name?" I ask him.

"My name is Martin," he answers.

"Well, Martin, nice to meet you. I'm Coach Albano. I'm the head football coach."

"Nice to meet you."

"Do you want to join the football team?" I ask him.

"Well, sir, thank you, but... I don't know anything about football, he says to me.

"It doesn't matter. We can teach you," I tell him.

"But I really don't know ANYTHING. Ha, ha!"

"It really doesn't matter. I can see that you have a strong leg, and that is exactly what we need. Are you interested? I ask him.

The boy is not that tall and might not weigh much, but he has a strong leg and the necessary precision to kick.

The boy is doubtful.

"Martin, if you want, I can talk to your father," I tell him.

"Uh, no. I will talk to him. Thank you."

Martin doesn't say anything for a moment. Finally, he says to me:

"Coach Albano? I'm interested but..."

"What's wrong, Martin?"

"I'm nervous," he says.

"I'm a little nervous, too," I tell him. "Don't worry."

Chapter 3
Jamal

"Jamal, come here, please."

"Sure, Coach Albano, just give me a second. I'm putting my pads on."

It's almost impossible to put on my practice jersey over my pads. Some of my teammates have to help me.

"Why is Coach Albano calling you?" a teammate asks me.

"I don't know. Let's go find out," I tell him.

I walk towards Coach's office. When I get there, I see a short, scrawny boy. He's probably five feet and six inches tall, maybe 140 pounds. He doesn't say anything.

"Jamal, meet Martin. He's our new kicker," Coach Albano tells me.

I don't say anything. I don't answer.

This kid is going to play football? Ah...., no.

"His name is Martin. You're going to help him with his helmet," Coach tells me.

Mr. Albano hands me a helmet for Martin.

"Well, say 'hello' to your new teammate," he says.

"Uh, Sure. Hi, I'm Jamal," I say to Martin.

We shake hands.

"Hi, Jamal."

"Jamal, I want to talk with you. Martin, Jamal is going to help you in a moment," Coach Albano says.

"Martin, wait for me. I will help you with the helmet in a moment," I tell him.

Martin leaves the office.

Is he nervous? He has to be nervous. He's so small!

Coach Albano starts talking:

"Jamal you're the team captain. Talk to the team. They need accept Martin. We need him."

"Okay, Coach. I'll talk to the guys," I tell him. "Can Martin play football?" I ask.

"We need him, Jamal. There is no one that can kick, and we need to win games..." Coach Albano is concerned.

"Coach, are you okay?" I ask him.

"Jamal, we need to win."

"Of course, Coach. We're gonna[4] win," I tell him.

Coach Albano is worried, but he asks me one more question: a question that is not about football.

"Jamal, you know that you can't play football if you don't have good grades."

"Yeah, I know," I say.

---

[4] gonna: going to.

"Are you going to have any trouble with your classes?" he asks me.

My classes...

I'm not such a good student. I like school, but I don't like to study much. And my classes are horrible...

"Spanish class? It's your second time taking that class, right?" Coach asks me.

Ugh! Spanish class. It's true that I'm not such a good student, but I'm a horrible Spanish student.

"Don't worry, I'll get a good grade in that class," I tell him.

Jamal, lying is not a good idea. Don't lie to Coach! I think to myself.

"Jamal, you need good grades in all your classes this semester. You are the quarterback and the team captain. We need you, and you need a scholarship," he says to me.

Spanish. Why is it so hard for me?

"Go help Martin. You are a leader, Jamal. Thank you. I will help you with the scholarship, but you also have to do your part," he tells me.

"Yes, sir. We're gonna have a great season," I tell him.

There's a lot of pressure and stress this season.

But it's true, I need a scholarship. I need a scholarship for college.

I leave Coach Albano's office.
I'm under a lot of pressure and have a lot of stress.

Chapter 4
Martin

As I'm leaving Coach Albano's office, I hear a bit of the conversation.

Coach is talking to Jamal about his grades, especially about his grade in Spanish class.

Ha. Spanish class. It's not hard for me. We speak Spanish at home.

But I have other problems, specifically with my father...

Jamal walks up to where I am and introduces me to the guys; I mean, men. They are huge.

"Guys, this is Martin. He's the new kicker for the team," Jamal tells them.

A really big kid — at least 250 pounds — speaks first:

"Him? He's going to be the kicker? My dog weighs more than him."

Another player agrees but makes no comments about my weight. He barks at me.

"You're going to be a football player? Hm. Then why do you have a soccer ball in your hands?"

"Boys, head to the field. Leave Martin alone," Jamal tells them.

I think about my soccer ball, and the conversation I had with my father before school in the morning.

Me: Bye, Dad. See you after practice.
Father: Martin, where is your soccer ball? You need it for practice, right?
Me: Oh, yeah thanks.
Father: Practice hard. When is the first game? I'm really excited to watch you play.
Me: Thanks. I don't know. I'll ask Coach today.

Ugh! I lied to my dad. I didn't mention the soccer team, or the football team.

Now, I'm in the locker room with teammates who are huge. I'm starting my new sport today.

With my shoulder pads and helmet, I walk towards the field. I can barely walk with all this equipment. I feel ridiculous.

I get to the field.

"Martin, come here," Coach Albano says to me. "We're going to practice special teams later. For now, work with Olaga. Olaga will teach you how to kick the football."

Olaga is not as huge as the other players, but he is still big.

"Come on, Martin," Olaga tells me. "Watch and learn."

Special teams? There are different teams on one team?

Steps for kicking? It's not just kicking the ball?

I don't know anything about football.

The lesson that Olaga gives me on how to kick the ball is easy.

I think about the steps:

1. From the tee, take three, medium steps back.
2. Take three, medium steps to the left (because I kick with my right leg).
3. Don't be too close or too far from the ball.

Olaga takes the ball and places it on the tee.

"Okay, Martin. Kick it," he tells me.

I accelerate towards the ball and kick it with a lot of strength. The ball flies.

"Wow...Martin! You know how to kick! For a small guy, you have a lot of strength in your leg."

Olaga is super happy and so am I.

"Guys, look! We have a kicker. Do it again, Martin!"

All the boys and coaches stop what they are doing to watch me. I kick the ball several times. With each kick, the ball flies.

Jamal walks up to me.

"Your kicks are phenomenal, Martin. The ball flies almost 50 yards (46 meters)."

Jamal shakes my hand for the second time.

"Martin, welcome to the team."

Chapter 5
Coach Albano

I'm in my office before practice. The game is in four days.

I look at my phone and notice that I have a new email from Mr. Moulton

Steve,
I look forward to the game on Friday.
Nik

I don't want to think about the game. I have another problem. I call Jamal.

"Jamal, come here, please."

At that moment, I see Martin.

"Hi, Martin. Are you ready for practice?"

"Hi, Coach Albano. Yes, I'm ready."

Jamal comes into the office.

"Jamal, your Spanish teacher sent me another email today. Your grade is horrible already."

"Coach, my grade is horrible because I'm horrible at Spanish," Jamal tells me.

"Jamal, you have to get a good grade. If you don't have a good grade..." I say to him.

Jamal is furious.

"Coach, I have good grades in the rest of my classes. Why do I need good grades in all of my classes? Ugh!"

Martin enters the office.

"Coach, I think I can help," Martin says.

"With what?" I ask Martin.

"Coach, I speak Spanish. I can help Jamal... if you want."

I look at Jamal. He's not furious anymore.

"What do you think, Jamal? Do you want help from the rookie kicker?" I ask him.

"Coach, I need help and if Martin can help me…"

"I can help you, Jamal," Martin says.

Yes! A solution to that problem, but we still need to win the game.

"Martin, thank you for helping Jamal," I say to him.

"No problem, Coach. Thank you for giving me a chance with the team. I still have a lot to learn."

"Martin we all still have a lot to learn in life. Did you talk to your father?"

Martin lowers his head. He doesn't say anything.

"Martin? Did you talk to your father about being on the football team?" I ask him.

He still doesn't say anything.

"Martin, it's a shame. It's a shame that you aren't playing soccer but it's not the end of the world."

"But my dad loves soccer. He has a dream of watching his son play professional soccer."

"I understand Martin. I have sons, too."

"Do your sons play football?" Martin asks.

"Oh, no, no, no. One of them is an artist, and the other plays golf."

"It's not a problem that they don't play football?" Martin asks me.

"Martin, my sons are wonderful. They are happy, good people. If they are happy, I'm happy."

Martin doesn't say anything.

"Martin, give me your father's phone number. I'm going to explain it to him, father to father."

Martin gives me the phone number.

"Thank you, Martin. I'll call him now."

"Thank you, Coach. I'll go get ready for practice."

I'm going to resolve another problem. I'm going to talk to Martin's father.

I dial the number.

"Good afternoon, Mr. Ortega? I'm Steve Albano, the head football coach."

Chapter 6
Jamal

AH! I have a speaking assessment in Spanish class. It's my second time taking the class because I didn't pass the first time. I need to get a good grade in the class this year. I need to pass...

"Hey, Jamal."

Martin enters the classroom.

"Are you ready to practice some Spanish?" Martin asks me.

"Hi Martin. Yeah, man. I'm ready. I have to get a good grade on this assessment."

"It's a speaking assessment, right?"

"Yes. I'm horrible at Spanish. I can't speak it at all," I tell him.

"Don't worry. I'll help you."

I look at the rookie kicker. Five foot nothing, 140 pounds, and 14 years-old, but he has confidence.

"What do you have to talk about?" Martin asks me.

"'My favorite sport'," I tell him.

"And you're going to talk about football, right?"

"Of course."

I see a look of terror in Martin's face.

"What's wrong, Martin?" I ask him.

"Oh Jamal, I don't know anything about football. I don't know if I can help you," Martin says.

"Martin, this is a symbiotic[5] relationship. You know Spanish, and I know football. I will explain football to you, and you help me with the Spanish. Okay?"

"Sounds good."

I spend some time explaining football to Martin. I tell him about:

---

[5] symbiotic: mutually beneficial.

- The number of players on the field and the rules of the game.
- The specific offensive and defensive positions.
- How to score, and how many points a touchdown, a field goal and a safety score.
- How long the game lasts.
- What plays the offense, defense, and special teams run.

I talk easily about my favorite sport. I love football. Martin listens attentively.

"Ok, Jamal. Now, I'm going to explain football in Spanish. Listen to my explanation. You're then going to explain the sport to me in Spanish."

"Okay," I say to him.

Martin explains in Spanish:

"In the sport of football, there are eleven (11) players on the field. When the offense has the ball, the players have four chances to move the ball ten yards. Each chance is called a 'down'. The objective of the game is to get to the end zone to score six points. The offense can run with the ball or pass it. The defense has to stop the offense in four downs to earn back possession of the ball."

Now I'm nervous. I understand Martin's words, but I can't speak. I don't have the words in Spanish.

I'm not going to pass the assessment.

"Okay, Jamal. It's your turn. Tell me about your favorite sport."

"Martin, man. I can't. I can't explain it in Spanish."

"What's the problem?" he asks me.

"I can't speak Spanish."

"Don't worry. Don't panic," he tells me. "What are you afraid of?"

"I understand it when you speak, but I can't use those exact words."

"Jamal, you don't have to use those exact words. Use your own words."

"My words?" I ask him.

"Yeah, don't think too much. Just talk. There is no communication if you don't use words."

This rookie kicker is right. But I'm still nervous...

"Okay, Jamal. Let's start with some questions. Question one: how many players are on the field during the game?"

"Oh, that's easy." In Spanish, I say, "There are eleven players on one team and eleven on the other. One team plays offense and the other plays defense."

"Good! Jamal, you're doing great!" Martin asks me another question: "How do you score points?"

"Easy. The offense must get the ball to the end zone. Then they score six points with a touchdown."

"Are there any other ways to score points?" Martin asks.

"Yes. After scoring a touchdown, the team can score an extra point. That's your job, Martin."

"Excellent Jamal! You speak Spanish well. Are there any other ways to score?"

"Yes. The kicker can kick the ball through the posts for a field goal. A field goal is three points."

"When do you kick the field goal?" Martin asks.

"A coach uses a field goal when the offense is close to the end zone, but a touchdown is not possible."

"Jamal, What's a 'down'?"

It's absolutely incredible: I'm speaking Spanish.

"Martin, a 'down' is a chance to move the ball ten yards or more. The offense has four downs to move the ball. If the ball is advanced ten yards, or more, the offense is awarded four new downs."

Martin listens to me. He helps me with a few words, but most of the time, I am explaining football — in Spanish!

"Thanks, Jamal! Now, I understand a little bit more about your favorite sport, and I understand the role of the kicker."

"Martin, you're a phenomenal tutor. Thank you. Now, I have confidence. I think I'll pass the assessment."

"You speak well Jamal. Don't be afraid. Use the words that you know. And if you don't know a word, just use the words you know to express an idea."

"We're a good team, huh?" I ask the rookie kicker.

We are a good team.

Chapter 7
Martin

"Martin!" my father calls to me.

"I'm coming!"

With my soccer ball, I go find my father.

"Good morning, Dad."

"Martin, what are you doing with the soccer ball?"

"To use it during practice..."

"Martin, I already know that you're not part of the soccer team. The coach called me."

"The soccer coach?" I ask him.

"No, the football coach. Coach Alberto..."

"Coach Albano." I tell him.

"Yes, Coach Albano. He told me that you're the kicker for the team. He said you have an excellent leg for plays that require a kick."

"Yes, Dad. I kick the ball, like it's penalty in soccer."

"Ah, I understand. But why didn't you tell me?" he asks me.
"Dad, you love soccer…"

There is silence.

"Martin, I love all sports. Now I can watch you play football!"

"Really? You're not mad?"

"No, of course not. But I don't understand…"

"What don't you understand?" I ask my father.

"Football, I don't know anything about it."

"Me neither! I'm learning."

"Explain to me what you do know."

I go to my room to get a piece of paper. I draw a football field: 100 yards.

"For your first lesson, Dad, I'm going to explain my role on the team. I'm part of the special teams.

"Special teams? All the players are on the same team, right?" my father asks.

It's obvious that my father has a lot to learn, like me. I show him a video.

"Watch this video. This is a play after a touchdown. The kicker has the chance to score a point. It's called an extra-point attempt."

"What is a touchdown?" my father asks.

"A touchdown is when a player with the ball in his hands reaches the end zone to score six points."

"Okay, Martin. Tonight, we'll have another lesson. Now, go to school."

"Okay, Dad."

I get my backpack and my soccer ball — without thinking — and start walking towards the door.

"Martin, leave the soccer ball here. You're a football player now."

My father smiles.

I smile, too, as I walk out the door.

Chapter 8
Jamal

It's time to eat — my favorite time of the day — and I'm with the boys. They are friends and teammates.

One of them has the nickname of 'Tank' because he's enormous. He weighs almost 300 pounds and is six feet and four inches tall. Obviously, he's an offensive lineman.

Another kid has the nickname of 'Bear' because he's a receiver and has enormous hands, like a bear.

We talk about the opening game. It's in two days.

"What do you think?" I ask them. "Do you think we're gonna win on Friday?"

"Of course," says Bear. "You throw the ball, and I catch it. The other team doesn't have a chance."

Tank doesn't say anything because he's focused on the other side of the cafeteria.

"What's wrong, Tank? You don't have anything to add? Normally you don't stop talking," I say to him.

"Look, near the door. It's that kid, Moulton, intimidating the new kicker."

Bear and I look toward the other side of the cafeteria. Ian Moulton, a junior, is intimidating Martin. Tank gets up.

"Tank, sit down. I'll deal with it."

"We're going with you, Jamal," Bear says.

"No. Sit down and stay here. I'll go."

I walk towards where Ian and Martin are. Ian is a teammate, but he's not my friend. He's a bully. He thinks highly of himself because his dad is the director of the board of education.

"Hi, Martin… Ian, what's going on here?"

Martin looks at me with fear in his eyes.

"Nothing's going on, Jamal. We're talking about the game," Ian says.

"Ah, really?"

"Yeah. We're talking about how we have to win the game or else…"

"And you think that if we win or not, it's Martin's responsibility?"

"I just want to remind him of his responsibility," Ian says.

"Moulton, don't be a fool. You know that each player has to do their job on every down to win."

"I know. EVERY player…" Moulton says, looking at Martin.

"Martin is going to play well. Leave him alone. Go to class."

"Fine, I get it. I'm leaving."

I look at Martin and I tell him, "Don't worry about him. He's a fool. He's insecure because he doesn't have the talent that Bear has."

"Thank you, Jamal. I don't know why he…"

"Don't panic, Martin. You're going to play well. Are you nervous?" I ask him.

"Yes and no. There's a lot of pressure that comes with being the kicker."

"With the quarterback as well. Even more pressure if I don't do well on the speaking assessment today."

Martin looks and me and says:

"Jamal, you're going to do fine. Football is your passion. Don't look for the perfect words, use the words that you know."

"Martin, you're really wise, you know? What happens if I don't know the correct words?" I ask him.

"Jamal, do what you do on the field, juke[6]."

"Ha, ha! That's funny. But it's a good idea. See you later, Martin. At practice."

"Good luck with the assessment."

---

[6] juke: a fake movement in sports to mislead an opponent.

Chapter 9
Coach Albano

The players are getting ready for practice. They put on their pads and their cleats.

The teens talk about everything: classes, their friends, and tomorrow's game.

"I can't wait for the game. We're gonna win." one of them says.

"Me neither. With our defense..." another one says.

"And with our new offense..." another one joins in "...we have a lot of potential."

I listen to my players with a smile. I love teenagers, and I love football.

I listen to the conversation between Jamal and Martin.

"Jamal, how did the speaking assessment go?" Martin asks.

"Martin, you're a phenomenal tutor. Thank you for the help," Jamal says. "I spoke really well."

I hear a handshake between the boys. Good, Jamal is going to be able to play tomorrow.

At that moment I get a notification on my phone. I have a new email from Nik Moulton:

> **Steve,**
>
> **We're going to win, and my son is going to play.**
> **Do you understand?**
>
> **Nik**

That guy. His son, Ian, is a good player, but has a horrible attitude. He can't play with that attitude...

It's time for practice.

"Ok boys. Get yourselves to the field. We're going to start in five minutes.

*****

Today's practice is a disaster.

"Do it again!" I tell them. "The offense is terrible."

I talk to Jamal and Ian:

"Jamal, look for Ian."

"Yeah, Jamal. I can't catch the ball if you don't…" Ian says.

"Shut up, Ian. You need to do your job, too," I tell him with a stern stare.

I'm worried. My job is at risk. If we don't win tomorrow, I'm not going to have this job, a job that I love.

"Tomorrow, we have to win! Do it again! This play has to be perfect."

The boys don't say anything. They understand that I'm worried and respond by playing well for the rest of practice.

"We'll finish with special teams work. Martin and Olaga it's your turn."

The guys on special teams jog onto the field. They practice kickoffs, field goals, and extra points. Martin must be nervous. He kicks badly, really badly.

"Martin, pull yourself together and kick the ball hard."

"Yes, Coach."

We practice some more kicks and end practice. I need to talk to the players.

"Boys. Come here." The players gather and take their helmets off.

The players kneel.

"Listen. We didn't practice well today, but tomorrow is another day. Tomorrow IS the day. Go home. Eat well. Drink water and sleep. Tomorrow is a test."

Now Jamal talks to the team.

"Boys. Tomorrow is the day. We're going to show our strength and ability. Listen to Coach. Drink water and sleep. We're going to win."

The boys start to yell with excitement.

"Let's go Tigers! Tigers! Tigers!"

I hope they are ready for tomorrow.

Chapter 10
Martin

We're about to run through the tunnel and take the field. I see a lot of people in the stadium. I'm very nervous.

As the captain, Jamal will go onto the field first. All the players, with their pads and helmets on, will follow. At that moment, Ian Moulton is next to me. He grabs my shirts and tells me:

"I need you to play really well tonight, do you understand?"

The other players see him, but they don't hear him.

But Coach Albano hears him.

"Ian! Come here!"

Ian goes to talk to Coach Albano.

Now Jamal says:

"Ready, boys? Let's go!"

As a team, we run behind Jamal onto the field.

The noise is terrifying and exhilarating at the same time.

Suddenly I hear my name 'Mar-Tin' 'Mar-Tin' and I see my father. I smile at him.

My father is with another man, a big man with a notebook. Who is he?

I also see Coach Albano talking with someone. The man must be Ian's father because they look alike. Neither Ian's father nor Coach Albano looks happy.

We finish with our warmup and begin to shout.

"Ti-gers! Ti-gers! Ti-gers!"

"Let's go, boys!" Coach Albano says. "Let's win!"

*****

The first half of the game goes by fast and slowly at the same time. We play well in the opening half. Jamal and the offense move the ball, but we don't get near the end zone to score.

The noise from the crowd is loud.

"Pass the ball! Pass the ball!"

"Coach, we have to pass the ball. They can't defend the pass. Their defensive is bad," Jamal says.

"Jamal, I know. But Ian can't play right now because of his attitude."

"Coach!"

"Jamal, we'll be fine."

I look at Ian. He's far away from Coach Albano on the sideline. He must be frustrated.

At that moment, San Marcos scores a touchdown. The crowd screams. The band plays their school's song.

After a successful extra-point, the score is 7-0 San Marcos at halftime.

Ugh!

*****

During the twelve minutes of halftime, we're all in the locker room. There is a lot of frustration.

Coach says:

"Boys, great job on the defensive side. But we have to do better offensively."

Again, Ian is at my side.

"We at least have to give Martin an opportunity to kick the ball."

"Ian! Leave him alone," Coach Albano says.

"Don't bother him. Martin is going to kick well in the second half."

"Coach, don't worry. Ian is encouraging me," I say.

Ian pats me on the shoulder.

"Kick well, man," he tells me.

*****

The second half starts slowly. We still can't move the ball into field goal range.

"Let's go, tigers!"

"Let's go, boys!"

Finally, Coach Albano yells to Ian, "Moulton, be ready!"

Jamal and Ian talk a bit on the sideline. Jamal passes the ball to Ian in in two downs we gain twenty-five (25) yards. Nice!

"Florida 22," yells Coach Albano.

I don't know what "Florida 22" is, but Ian runs so fast up the field as Jamal passes him the ball. I don't know how, but the ball arrives directly in Ian's hands.

Touchdown!

Yes!!!!

Yikes! It's my turn!

I jog onto the field and Olaga, the holder, tells me:

"You're ready, Martin. Don't worry. Just kick the ball."

Olaga grabs the ball and I kick it through the goal posts. Extra point!

Everyone pats me on the helmet. "Good job, Martin!" they tell me.

I'm excited, but the score is still 7-7 until the final minutes of the fourth quarter.

We're all nervous. Jamal has to be nervous because there are recruiters from universities watching him play. Coach Albano has to be nervous because he's the coach. I'm nervous, too, because there is only one minute left in the game.

Coach Albano calls me over.

"Martin! Come here!"

"Yes, Coach."

Martin, we're going to get close to the end zone and then it will be your turn. You're going to kick like we've practiced, okay?

"Yes, Coach."

The moment arrives.

"Martin, it's your turn," he says to me.

I run onto the field and hear my name:

"Mar-TIN! Mar-TIN!" Everyone is yelling for me.

Olaga talks to me again:

"Do it the same way you did before."

"Yes, sir," I say to him.

There are twenty-three (23) seconds left in the game.

I look to where my father is, and I smile.

The play is on the line of scrimmage on the 25-yard line. I take three steps back and three steps to the left. I'm farther away from the posts than in practice...

Suddenly, the ball flies into Olaga's huge hands. He grabs it and I take two steps and...

BAM!

Once again, the ball flies into the air and passes exactly between the posts.

A field goal!

People yell loudly. They yell my name again: "Mar-TÍN! Mar-TÍN!"

We win!

Chapter 11
Narrator

On the field after the game, Martin's father finds him.

"Martin! That was phenomenal! I'm so proud of you!"

Martin smiles.

"Thanks, Dad."

"Martin, can you get Jamal? This man wants to talk to him."

"Yeah, give me a moment."

Who is he? Is he a recruiter? Martin thinks.

"Jamal, over here!"

"Martin, you kicked really well! Nice job!"

"Thank you, Jamal. I want you to meet my father...and another man."

Jamal and Martin walk to where Martin's father is.

"Jamal, this is my father. Dad, this is Jamal, the quarterback of the team."

Jamal starts talking to Martin's father in Spanish.

Everyone is surprised.

"Is there a problem? I speak Spanish well. I have a good tutor," Jamal says, giving Martin a pat on the shoulder.

The mysterious man speaks:

Jamal, I'm Mr. Walkins. I'm one of the offensive coaches at UCONN. Here's my email and phone number. Call me. You're an excellent player."

Yes, sir! Thank you."

"And you," Mr. Walkins says to Martin, "continue practicing. You have a lot of potential.

"Thank you, Mr. Walkins!"

Suddenly they hear a loud voice.

"Albano!" Mr. Moulton yells. "Albano, come here!"

Mr. Moulton is close to Coach Albano and his face is very red.

Ian runs towards his father.
"Dad, don't say anything. Everyone played really well. Don't be mad."

"But," says Mr.Moulton, "you didn't play enough."

"No, I didn't play much. I didn't play much because I had a bad attitude towards Martin. I'm sorry Martin."

Martin doesn't say anything. It's not necessary.

"Dad," says Ian, "being angry is not necessary. We won."

Coach Albano speaks to Ian (and ignores Ian's father).

"Thank you, Ian. And Mr. Ortega, what do you think of your son?"

"He has a future in this sport. Thank you for helping my son."

"You're welcome. Now, boys, go celebrate in the locker room."

The boys run and yell, "Ti-gers! Ti-gers! Ti-gers!"

ABOUT THE AUTHOR

Jennifer Degenhardt taught high school Spanish for over 20 years and now teaches at the college level. At the time she realized her own high school students, many of whom had learning challenges, acquired language best through stories, so she began to write ones that she thought would appeal to them. She has been writing ever since.

Other titles by Jen Degenhardt:

La chica nueva | *La Nouvelle Fille* | The New Girl | *Das Neue Mädchen* | *La nuova ragazza*
La chica nueva (the ancillary/workbook volume, Kindle book, audiobook)
Salida 8 | *Sortie no. 8* | Exit 8
Chuchotenango | *La terre des chiens errants* | *La vita dei cani*
Pesas | *Poids et haltères* | Weights and Dumbbells | *Pesi*
LUIS, un soñador | *Le rêve de Luis*
El jersey | The Jersey | *Le Maillot*
La mochila | The Backpack | *Le sac à dos*
Moviendo montañas | *Déplacer les montagnes* | Moving Mountains | *Spostando montagne*

La vida es complicada | La vie est compliquée | <u>Life is Complicated</u>
La vida es complicada Practice & Questions (workbook)
El Mundial | La Coupe du Monde | <u>The World Cup</u>
Quince | <u>Fifteen</u> *| Douze ans*
Quince Practice & Questions (workbook)
El viaje difícil | Un voyage difficile | <u>A Difficult Journey</u>
La niñera
¡¿Fútbol...americano?! | Football...américain ?! | <u>Soccer -> Football??!!</u>
Era una chica nueva
Levantando pesas: un cuento en el pasado
Se movieron las montañas
Fue un viaje difícil
¿Qué pasó con el jersey?
<u>The Meaning You Gave Me</u>
Cuando se perdió la mochila
Con (un poco de) ayuda de mis amigos | <u>With (a little) Help from My Friends</u> *| Un petit coup de main amical |*
Con (un po') d'aiuto dai miei amici
La última prueba | <u>The Last Test</u>
Los tres amigos | <u>Three Friends</u> *| Drei Freunde | Les trois amis*
La evolución musical
María María: un cuento de un huracán | <u>María María: A Story of a Storm</u> *| Maria Maria: un histoire d'un orage*
Debido a la tormenta | <u>Because of the Storm</u>
La lucha de la vida | <u>The Fight of His Life</u>
Secretos | Secrets (French) | <u>Secrets</u> (English)
Como vuela la pelota
Cambios | Changements | <u>Changes</u>
De la oscuridad a la luz | <u>From Darkness into Light</u>
El pueblo | <u>The Town</u> *| Le village*

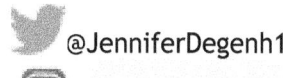@JenniferDegenh1

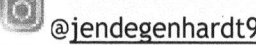@jendegenhardt9

@PuentesLanguage &
World LanguageTeaching Stories (group)

Visit www.puenteslanguage.com to sign up to receive information on new releases and other events.

Check out all titles as ebooks with audio on www.digilangua.co.

ABOUT THE TRANSLATOR

Susan Lopez is a 17-year-old student at Evergreen Charter School who is currently in 11th grade. She was born in Guatemala, on November 17, 2005. She arrived in the US in 2016 when she was 10 years old and now lives in Hempstead, New York. Susan is the oldest of three children. She's also a poet that has been published two times by the American Library of Poetry. Her favorite sport is badminton, and she loves to read. One of her favorite books is *Wonder* by R.J Palacio. Aside from writing poetry she's also a very talented artist. In the future she hopes to become a psychologist and help many people. Susan also wants to become a well-known author and poet.

ABOUT THE COVER ARTIST

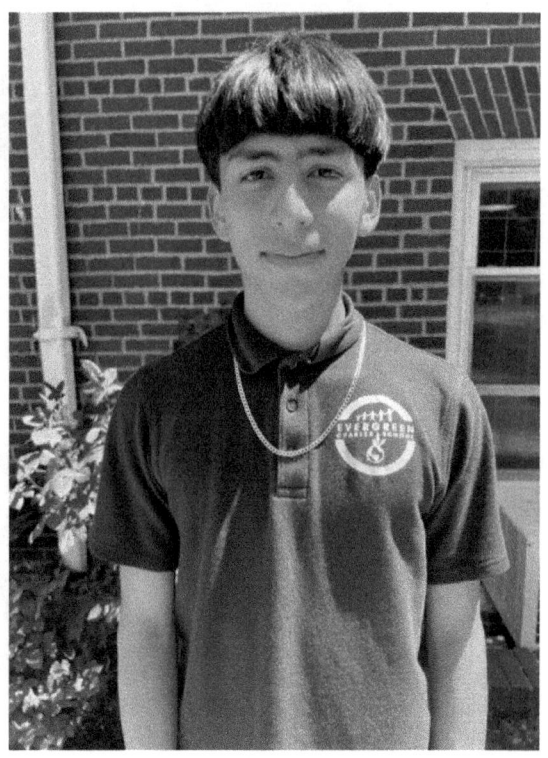

My name is Alex Duarte. I am 17 years old. I live on Long Island, New York, but I am from El Salvador, the country of pupusas and beautiful landscapes. I came to the United States a year ago, and have learned many new things, such as English and my passion for art, which is something I have really liked from a very young age.

ABOUT THE STUDENT LIAISON

Gracia Guzmán is a world Languages director at Evergreen Charter School. Her passions, teaching/learning and languages, combine to perfection in her role. She is originally from Spain, and she has been a language teacher in her home country, in the UK for over six years and in New York for the past five. She loves to travel, learn about different cultures and learn different languages to communicate with people from all over the world. She speaks English and Spanish fluently, French at an intermediate level, and she has been learning Portuguese for the past few years. Gracia Guzmán aims to enthuse her students to follow their dreams, to explore the world and to challenge themselves. In language classes, she tries to help their students to become world citizens who are culturally aware and responsive.

ABOUT THE EDITOR

Grant Collins, a rising junior at Bowdoin College (Brunswick, ME), was thrilled to be able to work on this project. As a Government/Legal Studies and Africana Studies double major, he was honored to bring his critical thinking skills to the editing process. As a college baseball player and lifetime athlete, Grant heavily contributed to the day-to-day sports lingo of the book. Grant hopes to pursue law school following college. He would like to thank his family, specifically his mother Amy, and brother Harrison, for always supporting him.

www.ingramcontent.com/pod-product-compliance
Lightning Source LLC
Chambersburg PA
CBHW060350050426
42449CB00011B/2913